Copyright © 2018 by Peter Wick

Cover Design and Interior by Ross Denyer

www. Peter-Wick.com

THE PAST IS GOING TO SUCK!

A TIME TRAVELERS GUIDE

THE 20TH CENTURY

BY PETER WICK

Table of Contents

Disclaimer #1	5
Disclaimer #2	8
Disclaimer #3	11
The 20th century, A brief overview	13
1900-1910	14
1910-1920	19
The Roaring Twenties	31
The 1930's	41
The 1940's	51
The 1950's	60
The Early 60's	67
The Late 60's	77
The 1970's	99
The 1980's	107
The 1990's	113
Final Thoughts	120
Photo Credits	122

Disclaimer 1: Don't make it worse!

The history of the 20th Century is all wrong.

Everything we know, all the famous historical events, are all mistakes. They are the result of careless time travelers trampling on the history they visit, altering it, and as a result, wiping out a nearly perfect, idyllic century in which war was nearly unknown, Hitler lived a quiet life as a bad painter, and The Cold War was a TV game show set in Antarctica.

The Cold War was a TV game show set in Antarctica

We at the Guide cannot stress this too strongly; please be careful with history. Once it is altered, no one, not even those who lived through it, will ever know any better.

This is not to say that the history of the 20th century didn't happen the way it is recorded here. It did. It just didn't happen that way when it actually happened.

Let us try to explain this another way.

This Guide tells the history of the 20th century, but it used to tell a very different history, and that very different history was of the 20th century…before it was altered….

You know what, never mind. We have decided to quit trying to explain this.

The point is, we must sadly accept the fact that the 20th century we are doomed to visit has been permanently changed from a near-perfect age, to the preposterous time that the history books now record.

So, please travel 'incognito,' and not 'interactive' (more on those options shortly).

Please! People! Do not make it worse!

It wasn't originally this bad. DON'T MAKE IT WORSE!

Disclaimer 2: How did this Guide come into existence?

(No, seriously, we want to know)

When the first primitive primates began using rocks as tools, they did not understand how the rock came to be in the first place.

Similarly, when world explorers navigated their sailing ships around the globe using stars as navigation tools, they did not fully understand exactly what the stars were, or how they moved through the sky. They only understood that their movements, when calculated accurately, helped them navigate.

Time travel is similar. We can do it.

We at the Guide have visited many eras – over and over – and we have done our best to guide you through your travels.

But…and we hesitate to admit this…we do not have any idea what we are talking about.

We blame you time travelers for this.

Whenever you alter something it only makes our job that much harder. You see, we do not know exactly how time travel works, and we are still discovering its long-term consequences.

If we are honest, we do not even know when we wrote this Guide, or when we re-wrote it.

…Or…when…or if…we even truly ever existed.

It all becomes very confusing, which is our whole point.

You see, time continues on into the future at the steady pace of one year per…well…per year.

Except when it doesn't.

And time travel – particularly the continuous altering of time, gets in the way of…um…TIME.

So, we want to say we originally compiled this Guide sometime in the 24th century.

But that's too simple a thing to say, especially when you consider that for a time, the 24th century itself was erased from history…or…erased from the future.

Our records suggest that at some point in the future – meaning the years after the 24th century – one of our many disgruntled readers – it turns out MOST of our readers are disgruntled – traveled back to the 24th century and erased it, and us.

Knowing this would happen (we can only ask you to accept that statement and move on), we sent several of our staff members into the past (and the future), with this Guide, to make sure it was carefully planted into existence at several different times in the past (and the future).

The problem, of course, is that this has made both the past and the future concepts that become somewhat vague and meaningless.

Time becomes meaningless…

This is complicated even further by our various staff members, who seem to have re-written parts of the Guide without our knowledge (well, we have eventually come to know this, or we will). So, we now speculate that there are infinite numbers of versions of history that have happened…or WILL happen, if you follow.

So, in the end, time, as a concept, is being ruined, by time travel…or will be ruined, or – as some theoretical historians prefer to say – "Will have never not be ruinated."

This is why we encourage all future (and past) time travelers to travel 'incognito.'

Disclaimer 3: Incognito travel versus Interactive travel

There are two ways you can visit other time periods.

Incognito travel allows you to land anywhere, anytime, observe the people and events, even listen in on private conversations. The only thing you can't do is talk to the people or interact with them.

Why? You are cloaked. You are incognito. They cannot see or hear you. They have no idea you are there.

We at the Guide would like to state for the record that we always recommend incognito time travel.

The other way you can travel, of course, is "interactively."

Interactive time travel is very enticing. It is tempting. It lets you talk to people. They see you. You can touch them. You can pretend to be one of them.

As we mentioned earlier, though, interactive time travel is destroying the whole idea of TIME.

We know! We get it. It's so much more fun to time travel in a way that allows you to talk and interact with people.

DON'T!

Please!

Okay, fine, we know you will anyway…but DON'T!

So, here is the history – one of the histories, anyway – of the 20th century, or at least one of the 20th centuries.

Did we mention how we hope you won't make it worse?

Yes? We're clear then? We understand each other? Okay.

The 20ᵗʰ Century – a brief overview

This guide focuses mostly on the history of The United States in the 20ᵗʰ Century.

The century, as it now exists, can be split into three basic periods, not of equal length.

The first period came first. It was followed by the second period, and we are still researching exactly when the third period happened.

The first 45 years (1900 to 1945) was a time of uncertainty and insecurity. Everyone, at least the vast majority of humans, were basically in pursuit of safety.

During the next 25 years (1945 to 1970) humanity realized that safety was an illusion, and instead pursued freedom and power.

Throughout the final 30 years (1970 to 2000) humanity just wanted a really hip place to hang out with friends.

We hope this loose outline helps you decide when and where you would like to visit.

1900 to 1910

The beginning of the 20th Century saw amazing advances in both technology and culture; the telephone, electric lights, movies, cars, airplanes. All were invented, and changed the way people lived, during this period.

Women were campaigning for the right to vote. African Americans were revolutionizing popular music. Rich white men were devising new and more efficient ways to exploit everyone on the planet.

It was the dawning of a new age.

It also gave birth to a new social phenomenon: old people who didn't understand new technology.

"What's the point of these newfangled contraptions?" they asked. "Things were fine the way they used to be. We rode horses and we were happy. We sent messages by carrier pigeon. We died at the age of 34 from something called 'gout,' and we were happy."

Between 1900 and 1910 nearly nine million people left the country of their birth and moved to the United States.

Most of the immigrants landed at Ellis Island, in New York, the site of the Statue of Liberty. It was here, under this grand symbolic tribute to 'liberty,' that they were given a nonsymbolic pathway to overcrowded tenement houses, crushing poverty, and entrenched racial battle lines.

This made their lives slightly better than they were back home.

In 1903 Orville and Wilbur Wright (back then people thought 'Orville' was a name. Now we know it is the sound you make when suffering from a bad digestive problem, rumors even suggest that his parents never intended to name him Orville, but that when his mother turned to his father and asked, "What shall we name him?" his father, who had just eaten a bad piece of sausage, did not even hear the question, and was bent over a bucket holding his stomach, uttering the sickly sound, "orville! orville!")…um, what were we talking about? Oh, yes…in 1903 Orville and Wilbur Wright flew the first motorized airplane. It flew about 120 feet, during which time a small snack of six tiny pretzels was served.

A small snack of six tiny pretzels was served.

If you are looking for interesting places to visit, San Francisco is always fascinating, but you'll want to get out before April 18, 1906. On this day, the great California tradition of surfing was born. Unfortunately, it was not yet applied to water. Instead, many thousands of San Francisco residents rode the waves of the Earth, as the ground shook and bounced.

This unidentified victim of the earthquake tragically loses his head and his balance at the same time!

The number one political figure during this decade was Teddy Roosevelt. He was famous for saying the word, "Bully!" when he liked something. Whenever someone told him some bit of happy news, he would smile and yell, "Bully!" Then he would gallop off on a horse. He was always galloping off on horses, which often caused problems during cabinet meetings.

He was always galloping off on horses.

Roosevelt started a new political party, which he called, "The Bull Moose Party." Looking back, this may seem like a poor choice for a name, but remember that it was a different time, with quaint cultural customs. Also, consider the names they rejected; The Cow Testicle Party, The Corrupt White Guy Party, and The Shut Your Pie Hole And Listen Party.

Culturally, the United States enjoyed everything from the 'high art' of Opera and Broadway Theater, to the 'low art' of Vaudeville comedians, and starving to death in Winter.

African American musicians Scott Joplin and Jelly Roll Morton were making 'Rag Time' and 'Jazz' the cool new music.

It would not be co-opted by white power brokers until at least 1907.

Scott Joplin and Jelly Roll Morton revolutionized popular music.

The first decade of the 20th century laid the foundation for all the absurd nonsense that would come later. It was just the beginning, though. Things would not get really awful for at least another four years.

1910 to 1920

In 1912 (we apologize for beginning the decade two years in, but after an extensive investigation, we have learned that, in fact, nothing actually happened in 1911 – many theoretical historians even suggest that the year never took place, that 1911 was skipped as being insignificant, and that the entire world moved directly from 1910 to 1912) a British ship company made the most amazing new ship imaginable.

It was called The Titanic.

It's builders claimed it was "unsinkable." Then they put it in the water.

As it set off on its maiden voyage, from England to New York, many rich socialites were on board, enjoying their rich socialite life, which, they were sure, protected them from anything bad happening. When a giant ice berg tore a hole the size of a giant ice berg in its hull, all the rich socialites were reminded that all the money in the world cannot protect you from being immortalized in a big budget Hollywood movie.

Nearly all of them died, which is a small price to pay in exchange for the world-wide fame of "going down with the Titanic."

Interactive Time Travel warning: If you visit the Titanic interactively, you are risking your own life. We cannot protect you from succumbing to the elements yourself. You take your life into your own hands.

AND....this is important....YOU MUST NOT WARN THE CAPTAIN OF THE ICE BERG.

If the Titanic does not sink, there is no telling what sort of time-altered consequences will ensue. First, history will lose one of its most important metaphors. Other unforeseen consequences may set a domino effect in motion so unpredictable that it may even result in causing the famous 1990's "Titanic" movie to star Johnny Depp instead of Leonardo Dicaprio. There are few fates worse than this known to humanity.

They claimed it was unsinkable...

...then they put it in the water.

After the Titanic sank, most people on Earth, surprisingly, were still alive. This meant they needed jobs.

Many workers found employment building the new machines that were changing the way people lived. Many of these workers discovered that the new 'assembly lines,' invented by

Henry Ford, paid well enough to provide a good living for their families.

Also invented, as a byproduct of Ford's assembly line, was the loss of one's soul and will to live, as workers got up each morning and trudged to work for another day of mindless repetition.

In 1913 Henry Ford brought to the world the first affordable mass-produced car, with his "Model T."

He should have stopped there.

Unfortunately, he also opened his mouth and spoke. This was a mistake.

You are wondering what he said? Let's just say that if you were Jewish, you might have considered buying from General Motors instead.

It took the public some time to get the hang of these new machines.

Meanwhile, in Europe, the continent's elite power brokers were getting angrier and angrier with each other.

Theoretical historians (those historians working to unravel history's original facts, before history was altered) believe these world leaders were originally able to resolve their differences. Once again, though, thanks to clumsy and careless time travelers, we have a much more troubling story to tell.

We will describe one time traveler's disastrous alteration of history, as both a warning and a caution.

This most devastating alteration of history happened in Munich, Germany, in 1913.

It happened when Sue Moody committed the one disastrous mistake that all time travelers must avoid…she tripped.

During the late Spring of the year 2172, Sue turned on the fusion reactor of her DX – 17 Toyota Prius Time Traveler, and set the date and location for October 16, 1913, in Munich, Germany.

She landed in a back alley, walked out to the main street, and tripped over a small child's foot.

She fell into a crowd of people, setting off a domino effect that toppled everyone for half a block. This included Kaiser Wilhelm, whose entourage was touring the neighborhood. Vladimir Lenin was visiting for the holidays (just which holidays we aren't exactly sure).

Also among the group was a 21 year-old gentleman who had just begun growing a funny mustache, and who liked to be referred to by the cute name, "Dolphie."

Though people were banged up a bit, most of the crowd bounced back to their feet uninjured.

The Kaiser, Vladimir, and Dolphie, however, had fallen awkwardly into each other. All three suffered minor concussions, and all three were treated at a local clinic. They suffered from blurred vision, headaches, and bizarre hallucinations.

Vladimir briefly believed he had become a small marmot. Kaiser Wilhelm believed for a time that he was a table lamp.

Kaiser Wilhelm believed he was a table lamp.

Dolphie got the worst of it. Suffering from extreme nausea and confusion. For several hours nurses worried that he would not recover. He believed fervently that he was a goat. He bleated at them without stopping until they gave him some shrubbery to eat.

"He wouldn't stop bleating," one nurse said, "until we gave him plants to chew on. Then he sat there, chewing sideways like a goat, staring at us. He went on like that for hours, until one of the doctors finally tried reasoning with him. Eventually he convinced him he was a human."

All three were eventually released, but confusion continued to plague them. It lasted for the rest of their lives.

Suffering from these confused cloudy thoughts, all three came to the unfortunate conclusion that killing lots of people and blowing things up would be a fun way to pass the time.

Dolphie's friends noticed a change in his personality.

Gone was the fun-loving and carefree youngster they had known. Self-deprecating humor was replaced by a tendency to shoot people.

Self-deprecating humor was replaced by a tendency to shoot people.

One childhood friend named Gunter sensed this change when he made a reference to a childhood memory. This was a reference that usually made Dolphie laugh.

This time, though, Dolphie ordered his henchmen to imprison Gunter. This tipped Gunter off to the possibility that something had changed.

Soon, the name 'Dolphie' was gone, replaced by the more formal 'Adolph.'

A year later, on June 24, 1914, Arch Duke Ferdinand, of Austria, was assassinated. This would cause the start of World War One.

You might wonder who Arch Duke Ferdinand was, and you might wonder why his killing would start a world-wide blood fest.

We refer you back to Sue Moody and her little tripping adventure, and remind you that very little in the 20th century made any sense after that.

Here is what happened, in quick succession:

Austria declared war on Serbia. Russia declared war on Austria. Germany declared war on Russia AND France (France was next door, Germany had noticed, and wars with neighbors are just lots of fun). England, feeling left out, declared war on Germany. Germany invaded Belgium. Luxemburg declared war on a small collection of pebbles. And…oh yes…it took a while, but eventually the United States declared war on Germany too.

Some historians also include a man in Yorkshire, England, who declared war on himself, but we think this is just taking it too far.

After four years of fighting, Luxemburg signed a peace treaty with the small collection of pebbles (they actually conceded some land to the pebbles).

As for the larger war, the United States, England and France finally won. The war was over.

It had been so much fun, though, that the three winning countries decided right away to begin laying the groundwork for the next one.

They made Germany sign a big stack of surrender papers. Germany was in no position to argue and signed everything without really reading it.

The Russians weren't at the big signing ceremony. They had pulled out of the war part-way through. They didn't think it was a good enough war and thought they could have a better one all by themselves.

The "Russian Revolution" was just Russia showing off. "Look," they said, "anyone can fight against another country. We're going to have our own war, by ourselves, killing our own people, and it will be better than yours."

Vladimir Lenin, who along with Dolphie and the Kaiser, suffered from that little concussion incident, was almost successful in upstaging Germany.

They overthrew their corrupt Czar family (or was that 'Tzar' or 'Csar' or 'Tsar' family?) and replaced them with NEW corrupt leaders.

In the end, a good half-century of future conflicts was set in motion.

Woodrow Wilson:

The United States' 28th President, Woodrow Wilson, brought the U.S. into the war, declaring that the war would, "Make the world safe for Democracy," and that it would be "the war to end all wars."

Everyone had a pretty good laugh about that.

After Germany signed their surrender papers, admitting that they lost the war badly, and promised to clean up the mess they had caused across Europe, Woodrow Wilson proposed that the winning nations form a 'League of Nations.' All future conflicts, Wilson said, would be settled by multi-national diplomacy.

Wilson was just full of these crazy ideas!

The rest of the world actually liked this League of Nations idea. The only people opposed to it were Wilson's own U.S. Congress. The League of Nations was doomed to failure before it ever got started. This laid the groundwork, though, for the United Nations, later in the century.

Basically, everything Wilson did in the year or so following the war had exactly the opposite effect he had intended; Germany would immediately begin planning their next, even more devastating war, future nations would forever boil over in conflict, and the world became about as safe for Democracy as a home full of foxes would be for their neighbors, the chickens.

Fitting neatly into this era of "Big fucking irony," was…

Prohibition:

In 1920 the United States banned the sale of alcohol, guaranteeing that thousands of people from coast to coast would become blinded and disabled by cheap, poorly made moonshine, sold in back alleys.

We suppose this means it is time to start the chapter on the 1920's.

The Roaring 20's

The 1920's was the decade when sex was invented.

Not that people didn't have sex before this. Obviously, no one would have existed if humans hadn't been having sex with each other.

Film star Clara Bow helped invent sex.

And (never start a paragraph with 'and' except this one) Sigmund Freud had been writing about how everything is about sex since the 1890's.

But (never start a paragraph with 'but' except this one) the 1920's was the first time that 'modern life' allowed for the excess and indulgence that would make sex the hip new thing.

The younger generation – those in their 20's in the 1920's – were called "The Lost Generation." It was the first time anyone had thought of naming a generation. Prior to the 1920's people just worked themselves to death desperately trying to survive. By the 1920's modern life had created enough leisure time that an entire generation had time to get lost.

Let's take a look at a few things time travelers might want to see.

The New York Stock Exchange:

Since computers did not exist yet, all stock trades had to be made by sweaty over-stressed brokers who lived on the floor of the Exchange, yelling, throwing slips of paper around and, at the end of the decade, throwing themselves out of a 15th floor window.

The 1920's was the heyday of overblown stock value.

The market was growing rapidly, and everyone wanted to get in on the action. They often borrowed money to invest. When the bubble burst in 1929 billions of dollars were wiped out overnight.

One unlucky man was given the job of cleaning up the New York Stock Exchange, after everyone else had jumped out the 15th floor window.

Speakeasies:

The law that made alcohol illegal in 1920 was really just a grand experiment to see if America's organized crime families could get their act together.

The experiment worked beautifully.

Those who illegally smuggled alcohol into the country were called "Bootleggers."

Others, who distilled their own alcohol in makeshift backwoods distilleries were called 'blind,' or in some cases 'dead.' This was the unexpected side-effect of drinking spirits laced with methanol.

Some desperate people even tried to drink paint thinner.

More common, though, were the secret underground bars and taverns known as 'speakeasies.' Every major city had several of them. This is where the smuggled alcohol – usually from that corrupt and overly drunk country, Canada – was served.

Al Capone was the country's most famous smuggler.

Capone was a Chicago-based gangster. He cultivated a number of Chicago traditions, especially that time-honored tradition known as the "Corrupt Politician." He turned corruption into an art-form, bribing Chicago's mayor to turn a blind eye while he built an empire of fear.

Two Chicago officials enjoying the new "corruption" that was

becoming so popular.

His reign of terror dominated Chicago during the second half of the 20's, ensuring that he would go down in history as the third greatest crime boss ever to be played on film by Robert Deniro.

We don't want to jump to the 1930's yet, except to say that in 1932 Al Capone was finally caught and thrown in jail, not for murder or bribery, but for tax evasion.

The third greatest crime boss ever to be played by Robert Deniro.

We do not advise you to visit Al Capone's Chicago interactively. It might seem daring and fun, but the bullets are a little too real.

A note about dying in the past

It is with concern and caution that we bring up a false theory about time travel that many travelers seem, sadly, to believe.

The theory suggests that it is okay to get killed in the past; you will eventually be born, just as you originally were, and then you can just avoid making the fatal mistake.

This is too simple a way to view things, though, and as we mentioned earlier, it is made even riskier by the fact that time is being ruined by time travelers.

One time traveler, Dean O'Malley is believed to have taken this risk, but in doing so, altered history just slightly. He failed to prevent his death on his second trip into the past, and went a third time, resulting in all three of him meeting himself (or should we say 'himselves') just before the fatal moment. This had the unfortunate effect of one of the 'hims' accidentally firing the fatal shot.

The end result of this circular chain of events, is that it turned out that it had always been the third him who had killed the first him in the first place. By the time he was born some centuries later he had also somehow become his own great great grandfather.

He continued to time travel, hoping eventually to find the right balance of himselves. Finally, he altered history in such a way that he accidentally wiped himself out of existence, meaning that none of this actually ever happened….in the current state of history. We mean, it happened. You just won't find any record of it happening, or of Mr. O'Malley ever existing.

Skeptics discount this entire incident as being absurd and silly, which it certainly is, but that doesn't mean it didn't happen. We mean, it didn't, but first it did. Thanks to careless and sloppy time travelers there are many incidents that both did and did not happen, and in fact, they did and did not happen simultaneously.

New York in the 1920's:

New York is a much safer place to visit than Chicago, as your death is much more likely to be caused by a random lone psychopath.

New York was the cultural and financial center of the time. Writers, artists, all manner of cultural movers and shakers, were based in New York. Perhaps the two greatest cultural movers and shakers were F. Scott and Zelda Fitzgerald.

Scott wrote the defining novel of the time, "The Great Gatsby." Zelda went insane. Together they symbolized the era.

Scott and Zelda Fitzgerald. He wrote the greatest novel of the decade. She went insane.

One of the more glamorous cultural phenomenons of the time was a group of writers and artists called "The Algonquin Roundtable." Famous faces, from writers to actors to socialites, all manner of artists, would gather for lunch at the Algonquin Hotel and try to outdo each other with witty comebacks.

Alexander Woolcott, Harpo Marx, Dorothy Parker, Robert Benchley, George S. Kaufman, Harold Ross – who founded The New Yorker Magazine in 1925 – were just a few of the names that gathered at the Algonquin. Others included playwright Noel Coward, and actress Tallulah Bankhead.

Art Samuels, Charlie MacArthur, Harpo Marx, Dorothy Parker, and Alexander Woolcott.

Famous put-downs were born here, such as George S. Kaufman's line, directed at a friend who he thought was out of town, "Ah, forgotten but not gone," (rumored to have been borrowed many years later by President John F. Kennedy) and Dorothy Parker's, "I never liked a man I didn't meet."

If you plan to visit the Algonquin interactively, hoping to bask in erudite wit, just remember that the sharp dagger of wit can quickly turn against you. A slip of the tongue could backfire, resulting in a devastatingly sarcastic critique of 'future boy.' We aren't suggesting that suffering through a great wit's put downs would be as devastating as being shot by one of Al Capone's henchmen. There have been unconfirmed reports, though, of people leaving the Algonquin after suffering through a barrage of witty sarcasm, and later dying suddenly of embarrassment. Please be careful.

The 'Roar' comes to an end:

The "Roaring 20's" ended in spectacular fashion. A full decade of excessive borrowing and extreme indulgence came to a crashing end in 1929.

When the stock market decided to crash, it crashed in full out-of-control-space-cruiser-crashing-into-an-asteroid mode.

40 percent of the U.S. economy was wiped out. Thousands of banks closed their doors.

People who name time periods originally wanted to name the following years, "The depressing sad unhappy really bad no good depression." But the newly sophisticated advertising industry said no. "It has to be something 'Great,' a 'Great' something," they said. So, the period beginning as 1929 turned into 1930 was given the much catchier and zeitgeist-y title, "The Great Depression."

The 1930's

(Who knew a depression could be so great?)

The man who was President, as the 1920's ended and the 1930's began, was Herbert Hoover.

Hoover, a Republican, responded to the collapse of the nation's economy, the massive number of job losses, and the failure of thousands of banks, by eating steak for breakfast.

Hoover diverted from a long-standing American tradition of blindly throwing money at problems by…well….by NOT throwing any money…at the biggest financial problem the country had ever faced.

Millions of people lost their jobs, their savings, and their homes. They gathered in makeshift homeless communities that they called "Hoover-villes." President Hoover made the mistake of thinking this was a compliment.

By the time of the 1932 election a quarter of all workers were unemployed, the stock market had lost 80 percent of its value, and

Hoover's approval was at an all-time low. So Hoover did the only thing he could think of; he ran for re-election.

Hoover ran against Franklin D. Roosevelt, who ran on the catchy slogan, "Happy days are here again!"

By contrast, Hoover, who felt that the Great Depression was his single most important accomplishment, ran on the slogan, "Make the Depression Great Again!"

President Hoover, pretending he can't hear the protests of an entire nation...

...then he pretended he could run against this guy.

Roosevelt won easily.

His first order of business? Find the money Hoover didn't throw at the problem and…throw it at the problem.

Roosevelt had won the election by promising a "New Deal." He quickly passed legislation that made the federal government the biggest employer in the country. He increased the reach of the government's hiring and spending, investing in roads, bridges, and dams.

He asked the government to literally print more money and send it out to the banks.

It worked, but it didn't solve the entire problem.

While things had gotten better, much of the country was still living in crushing poverty in the middle of the decade.

Interactive cautionary tale from the 1930's:

Did we mention that we think you should not travel interactively? Yes? We mentioned that?

We have researched the events surrounding a railroad car full of 'hobos' in 1934. The train was traveling from Kansas City to California, with an estimated dozen men inside the square boxcar, hoping to eventually find farm work in California.

Among them was a traveler from the future named Warren Stanton. Stanton had taken the trouble to look like one of the hobos. He had grown his beard out for several weeks, avoided showering, and took on the physical habits and accent of the men he traveled with,

The men, naturally, suffered from extreme nagging hunger.

Late at night, when Warren assumed the men were all asleep, he removed a turkey club sandwich from his bag.

One of the men opened his eyes as Warren took his first bite.

What happened next is still open to speculation, but we know for certain that Warren did not survive the incident.

Hollywood in the 1930's:

With much of the country suffering from crippling poverty, and in many cases living in cardboard-house shanty towns, people saved what money they could scrape together for the really important things, like…going to the movies.

The 1930's are considered the beginning of Hollywood's golden age.

Stars such as Clark Gable, Fred Astaire, Ginger Rogers, William Powell, Myrna Loy, Cary Grant, Katherine Hepburn and James Stewart became celebrities. They offered escapist stories about wealthy high society people that the penniless masses ate up as fast as Hollywood could churn them out.

William Powell and Myrna Loy, offering the poverty-stricken masses hope that they could spending their last pennies gawking at glamorous STARS!

Re-election:

In 1936 the Republican Party nominated someone to run against Franklin D. Roosevelt. They had to. That's how political parties work.

Their nominee was named Alf Landon. The reason they nominated someone named Alf Landon is that by 1936 the Republican Party had gone completely insane.

While the economy had still not fully recovered, Roosevelt's "New Deal" had at least stabilized things, and much of the country felt confident that the slow steady progress would continue.

In response, the Republicans said, "We're doomed. Let's nominate someone with a name that sounds like a cartoon character!"

Alf Landon then went on to campaign – check that, he hardly campaigned at all. When he did campaign he accidentally voiced approval for Roosevelt's New Deal. In fact, campaign advisors had to stop him from putting out negative ads against himself.

"Why?" he asked. "I thought that when you are behind in the polls, you have to go negative."

"Yes," his advisors agreed, patiently, "you have to go negative…against the other person, not against yourself."

"Oh!" Alf said. "Sorry."

Roosevelt won with a tally of 523 Electoral votes to Landon's 8.

Alf Landon visits the White House to personally thank Roosevelt for crushing his soul.

By the late 1930's the Great Depression was definitely losing its greatness.

With the economy chugging along, people began turning their attention to more exciting things; It was time to bring back WAR!

Europe in the 1930's:

We at the Guide do not want to spend too much time discussing Europe. This is not to disrespect Europe. It's just that Europe gets too much attention anyway.

There were occasions during the 20th century, though, when things happening in Europe actually mattered.

Europe in the 1930's was a festering cesspool of military aggression.

Germany had elected the previously brain-damaged "Dolphie," who had changed his name to "Der Fuhrer, Adolph Hitler."

Always be wary of leaders who demand too much loyalty. That, plus grandiose names like "Fuhrer," plus funny hand salutes and comic mustaches. These things combined in one person will always spell trouble.

Hitler's grand plan was to conquer Europe and establish the blond Aryan race as the supreme world power.

It didn't work out very well.

Long story short:

Hitler was gradually building up his power base through the 1930's.

In 1936, he and Germany hosted the Olympics, where African American athlete Jesse Owens stuck it to the brain damaged mad-man by winning four gold medals.

Jesse Owens sticks it to Hitler.

In 1938 British Prime Minister Neville Chamberlain and several other European leaders met in Munich, Germany, to discuss Hitler's plans to take over parts of his neighboring countries. The European leaders did not want to go to war yet. They wanted to push that back a year or so, when their busy schedules would open up a little. With this scheduling crunch in mind they negotiated a very unique agreement.

Dolphie giving himself the one thing no one else ever gave him: a hug.

This agreement stated that, rather than muck things up with lots of fighting, Germany could take over land from their neighbors for free.

You read that right. Chamberlain negotiated a deal in which, rather than fight for neighboring land, Hitler could take it for free.

In a follow-up negotiation, Chamberlain offered to give all of his money and the clothes he was wearing directly to Hitler, asking for nothing in return but a small blue towel. Hitler declined the offer, and instead took all of Chamberlain's dignity and self-respect.

A year later, in 1939, Germany invaded Poland. The war was on.

This would be the BIG ONE!

The 1940's

In 1940 Franklin D. Roosevelt won a third term as President. He goes down in history as the only President ever to serve a third term. Several years after his death, Congress passed a law banning Presidents from serving more than two terms.

Before Roosevelt, Presidents considered a third term "un-Presidential."

Roosevelt, riding a wave of popularity unrivaled in the history of the Presidency, decided that not only was a third term 'Presidential,' it would also be really freaking awesome.

The only problem?

How to convince the American public to once again go to war against Germany.

He finally made his case by convincing the public that thousands of future war movies were at stake, that untold countless hours of not-yet-made "World War 2" movies hung in the balance and risked never being made if the United States did not enter the war.

We struggle to tell you when and where to visit in the 1940's because, well, just about anywhere you go you are likely to be slaughtered in the world-wide bloodbath.

Most places aren't so fun to visit in the 1940's.

It wasn't just Europe.

Japan had built an empire that included Korea, parts of China, and much of southeast Asia.

They could have just sat on this empire for years, without any fear of an equal military power challenging them.

That would have been too easy, though.

As often happens with ambitious military powers, they did the stupid thing.

They attacked Hawaii. They sank a large number of U.S. Navy ships.

Their hope:

Cripple the U.S. Navy so they could rule the Pacific Ocean unchallenged.

What they accomplished:

War with the United States.

Once again military ambition leads to crystal clear tactical judgement.

(Don't worry, we'll get to the USA's own bone-headed military ambition before this guide is finished.)

So…Japan attacked Pearl Harbor and sank several U.S. war ships.

The U.S. promptly declared war on Japan.

The question you may be wondering, though, is, how did this finally get the U.S. into the war in Europe?

This brings us to the single most idiotic decision resulting from insane military ambition, ever, in all of history.

The attack on Pearl Harbor, and America's declaration of war against Japan, could have just been a side war to Europe's main event.

BUT…remember Dolphie?

For no clearly understood reason, reportedly 'off the cuff,' Dolphie - ruler of Germany – declared war on the United States four days after Pearl Harbor.

With the 'sleeping giant' of the United States awake and mobilized, it was only a matter of time before they would vanquish all enemies.

It would still take four years to do it, but eventually the U.S. along with England, France, and Russia, claimed victory.

The Allies (it's important to have a good team name) invaded the coast of France on "D-Day" June 6, 1944, establishing the beginning of the end of German rule over Europe.

Allied ships approach the coast of France on "D-Day".

On May 8, 1945, Germany surrendered.

Dolphie shot himself, and the European stage of the war was over.

Three months later the United States became the only country ever to obliterate two entire cities full of civilians, when it dropped atomic bombs on Hiroshima and Nagasaki, Japan.

Japan surrendered.

The war was over.

TIME TO START THE NEXT ONE!

This was a very quick, very simplistic overview of the bloodiest war in human history.

It skips through so quickly that we have left out a few important details.

Franklin D. Roosevelt actually won a fourth election as President, in 1944. He was suffering from poor health, though, and died in March of 1945.

His Vice President, Harry Truman, succeeded him as President and oversaw the end of the war.

Also skipped in this overview was...everything else that happened.

The rapid build-up in manufacturing military equipment effectively ended the Great Depression.

Hollywood celebrities took a break from the frivolous act of making movies and joined the war effort. James Stewart – who had starred in the popular hits, "Mr. Smith Goes to Washington," and "The Philadelphia Story," did not make a movie for five years while he served as a war pilot. This example should answer the age-old question, "If I stop being famous do I also stop existing?" The answer seems to be no.

James Stewart and Clark Gable quit making films for a few years. Surprisingly they still existed.

Before we leave the war behind, we wanted to give you a list of…

Forgotten Battles of World War 2:

C-Day

A few months before the more famous "D-Day," several thousand U.S. troops invaded a popular pub on the south coast of England. Unfortunately, the pub was too small to hold them, and collapsed. The Americans declared victory over the pub and celebrated with the locals by ruthlessly drinking all the pub's leftover alcohol.

The Invasion of Italy

Many people do not realize that the Allies invaded Italy long before they invaded France. It is an understandable oversight, though, since the citizens of Italy had already turned against their despotic ruler, Mussolini, and thrown him in jail. The entire country was now in the mood for some Allied love.

King Kong versus Godzilla

One of the most epic battles of all time pitted America's beast ape against Japan's terrifying new monster. Do not believe the claims that Godzilla came into being only after the Atomic bomb was dropped. This epic battle took place on a remote Pacific island in early 1944. It was reported to be a stalemate. Those who have been lucky enough to witness the battle have described it as "Totally f---ing AWESOME!"

One of the epic battles of World War 2!

So…now it had become the late 1940's. The United States had unleashed a new era of fear and peril with their use of the atomic bomb.

The war was over, though.

What to do next?

Start the next one, of course.

The next one would be called, "The Cold War," and sadly would have nothing to do with playing croquet in Antarctica.

"The Cold War" lasted for more than 40 years.

The Cold War was less a war and more a tango between dance partners who hated each other.

Russia, in helping to defeat Germany as World War 2 ended, annexed just about all of eastern Europe, and called themselves The Soviet Union.

Once allies, The U.S. and the Soviet Union were now mortal enemies.

This might actually be a more fun time for time travelers to visit. Why? Most of the serious killing was over. Now it was SPY TIME.

Americans and Soviets settled into the coolest spy vs. counter spy game in all of history, with big name celebrities like James Bond getting involved.

Okay, Bond wasn't a real person, but you see how things were evolving. Instead of living in squalid conditions, in fox holes and trenches, suffering from disease, and enduring unspeakably harsh conditions, the combatants played cards in casinos, slept with beautiful double-agents, and sabotaged each other's diabolical plans. What's not to love?

But we are getting ahead of ourselves (a common problem when time traveling).

The Cold War was barely on yet in the late 1940's. First Russia had to catch up with the U.S. and build their own atomic bomb. Once that happened, in 1949, the real fun started.

The 1950's

The 1950's were either the most absurd period in the history of humankind, or THE BEST OF TIMES, to be revered and honored forever.

Let's break things down to make it easier to keep track.

He 1950's brought:

-The Korean War

-The Eisenhower Presidency

-Joe McCarthy

-Elvis Presley

-James Dean

-The Beat Generation

-Rosa Parks

-Television

-New coast to coast freeways

-A booming economy

-The Quarter Pounder with Cheese

All seasoned by the eternal daily threat of complete and total nuclear annihilation.

Where would you like to visit?

How about starting at a drive-in diner for some milk shakes. Then try a drive-in movie to make out in the back seat of your car with your 'main squeeze.' Then practice some "Duck and cover" to survive the coming nuclear apocalypse under your desk.

Very funny! Come on, people, this did NOT originally happen! Some sick practical joke played on the 20th century by time travelers....

The American economy was booming like no one had seen in decades. Gone were the poverty and hunger of The Great Depression. Cultural shifts saw a massive move to the suburbs, a massive belief in "The American Way," and a massive rejection of anything that challenged the American status quo.

And that status quo was growing into the consumer culture that would eventually impair the critical judgement of every living thing on the planet.

America's new booming economy needed people to go BUY THINGS whether they needed new things or not. Go shopping! Buy with credit! It's The American Way!

Buy new televisions!

Watch the new commercials splashed all over those televisions. Then go out and buy all the things you've seen ads for.

The popular "Howdy Doody" show.

Television made everything better!

Combine all these factors with the cold stand-off against Russia, and the door was opened for Senator Joe McCarthy and his "Un-American Activities" committee.

Anyone who questioned the 'American way' was hauled into McCarthy's committee and grilled for hours about the size of their love for America, and the depth of their hatred of communism.

Senator Joe McCarthy explains where the Commies are hiding.

Into this environment came the beginnings of a quiet underground protest movement.

It wasn't really a full movement yet. That wouldn't come until the 60's, but the foundation was being laid for later, more potent protests.

Rosa Parks became an iconic civil rights activist when she refused to give up her seat to white passengers on a Montgomery, Alabama bus.

Decades of black/white segregation had turned into entrenched institutional racism in the southern states. Activists like Parks, and the movement's leader, Dr. Martin Luther King, Jr., had the audacity to demand freedom and equality. They won an instant victory for these cherished American concepts and values, and…wait, hold on…nope! Sorry, that was from the original, more sensible and rational version of the century. They didn't win any instant victories. Weird! Now you might begin to see why the 60's had to happen.

Meanwhile, The Beats – writers such as Jack Kerouac and Allen Ginsburg – were writing in surprising and experimental new styles. Actors such as Marlon Brando and James Dean were revolutionizing cultural attitudes through film. Rock and Roll music was beginning to separate the new "Baby Boom" generation from their parents middle American attitudes.

In the 1953 film, "The Wild One," Marlon Brando's character, Johnny Stabler, is asked, "What are you rebelling against?" Brando's response, "What do you got?" summarized a pervasive new unfocused dissatisfaction.

When was time travel invented?

This is a difficult question to answer, because time travelers are always going back to some previous time period to help some scientist from the past 'invent' it before it was really invented.

Our best guess, after investigating real scientists from the past, is that time travel was invented in either 1955 or 1985 (most likely BOTH years simultaneously) by the great Dr. Emmet Brown, with the help of his assistant, Marty McFly.

If you have seen the popular movie of their adventures, "Back to the Future," you might be tempted to believe it was fictional. We can assure you that the events in the movie really happened, at least in one of the versions of the 20th century.

There is another version of these events in which Marty McFly stays in 1955, and actually goes to the school dance with the teenage version of his own mom. They fall in love and stay together. This is acceptable in some of the more open-minded versions of history, but can accidentally result in erasing the time traveler from existence.

Wrapping up the 1950's

People growing up in the 1950's thought they were living in the most amazing decade ever. America ruled half the world. Money was everywhere. God hated communists. TV shows made it possible for everyone to pretend they didn't live in a completely dysfunctional family. A new generation of energetic and creative youth was growing up. Music, film, and culture overall were changing in new and exciting ways. African Americans were expressing their right to equality and dignity. EVERYTHING was finally how it should be.

And if you believe that statement, you should not continue reading.

The early 1960's

Most decades of the 20th century can be discussed in a single chapter.

Not the 1960's.

This decade was so packed full of events and surprises, it was like two decades packed into one.

Let's begin in 1960 – a sensible place to begin, since it was the first year of the decade.

Throughout all of the prosperity of the 1950's, throughout all of the patriotic fervor, throughout all of that wonderfully contagious sense that America was tops in the world, there was one nagging, unsettling, unavoidable problem that the country just seemed unable to overcome; President Dwight D. Eisenhower, despite being a great man, despite being liked and respected worldwide, even after eight successful years in office, was still noticeably, undeniably…..BALD.

That, the country decided, would never happen again.

Sorry, Baldy, the 50's are over!

The torch has been passed to a handsomer, hipper America!

In 1960 American voters replaced the 70 year-old Eisenhower with 43 year-old John F. Kennedy.

As Eisenhower left office he gave a famous speech in which he warned America to be wary of what he called "the military industrial complex." He was right, of course. America's military industrial complex would hold the entire national budget hostage from that day throughout the remainder of time.

Thanks to television, America heard this warning, scrunched up their faces, said, "Whaaaa---?" and then switched to a different channel.

Kennedy suffered through an early catastrophe when he allowed a previously planned invasion of newly communist Cuba to proceed. It was called the "Bay of Pigs," and turned into a disastrous failure. The President and the CIA briefly toyed with the idea of a second invasion, to be named the "Harbor of Donkeys," but eventually dropped the plan. (Side note: This invasion would leave its most profound legacy years later in the naming of bands such as, "Flock of Seagulls," "Band of Horses," and the lesser known "Symphony of Yaks.")

President Kennedy and his wife Jackie – a superhuman female sent to Earth from a far superior planet – brought glamour to the White House for the first time since the glamour days of….you know what, these were the first and only glamour days the White House ever saw.

A superhuman female sent to Earth from a far superior planet.

Kennedy oversaw a tumultuous period of time; race relations in the southern states were beginning to boil over, the stand-off with the Russians brought the world to the brink of nuclear war, America was beginning to be drawn into a disastrous civil war in a small Asian country called Vietnam, and America's youth were beginning to show signs that they might one day actually think for themselves. How could these worrying trends be stopped!?

As for that 'brink of nuclear war,' comment, that was the Cuban Missile Crisis, and it made the world hold its breath in October, 1962.

Russia had installed missiles in Cuba, just 90 miles from the U.S. mainland.

Kennedy established a blockade, preventing all Russian ships from reaching Cuba.

The standoff lasted for 13 days and genuinely seemed to be the beginning of World War 3.

Cool minds prevailed, though. Kennedy and Soviet leader Nikita Khrushchev mutually backed down, giving Kennedy's critics fuel for criticism. Republicans were irate over the fact that the world was not at all blown up. How could a President live with himself in a world that was not blown up? A true leader would have pushed the button and ended everything. Kennedy was WEAK!

As for the growing civil rights movement, Martin Luther King, Jr. gave a famous speech on the steps of the Lincoln Memorial in 1963. "I have a dream!" he proclaimed. But too many Americans were living in a nightmare for his dream to have immediate effect.

In the end the Kennedy Presidency was doomed. It all came to an end in November, 1963.

Without going into too much detail, President Kennedy, this charismatic leader of this new generation, either was or was not shot by; a lone gunman, the CIA, the FBI, the Russians, the

Cubans, the Illuminati, his own Vice President Lyndon Johnson, some crazy loser who admitted it in a jail cell decades later, or all of the above…or none of the above (covering the possibility that his assassination was staged and that he secretly lived in an underground bunker until Elvis 'died,' and the two of them traveled the country incognito in the coolest secret road trip ever!)

Whatever actually happened, Lyndon Johnson was sworn in as President on an airplane that evening.

Johnson's first major act as President was to sign the popular Civil Rights Act of 1964. It was an astounding achievement, outlawing discrimination across many facets of society.

Johnson and Martin Luther King, Jr. made the Civil Rights Act a reality in 1964.

Johnson did a couple of good things, before completely destroying his Presidency with the Vietnam War.

Lyndon Johnson had always been an ambitious politician. It had irked him that Kennedy had beaten him for the 1960 Democratic nomination. Now he was President. Finally, his destiny was on course. It was now time to set in motion as many elements as possible, that would, within the next five years, completely derail his ambition, and bring his own Presidency crashing down. But FIRST?

The 1964 election.

In 1964 the Republican Party nominated Barry Goldwater to run against Lyndon Johnson. Why did the Republicans nominate Barry Goldwater? Because, once again, the Republican Party had gone completely and totally insane.

Goldwater was a very conservative Senator who believed it was okay to resort to 'extremism' in order to destroy communism.

Johnson responded by running the famous "Daisy ad," a television commercial showing a little girl playing with a flower, followed by footage of a nuclear explosion. The message was clear; Goldwater will kill us all. Johnson won a landslide victory. Southern conservatives, angry over the Civil Rights Act, sided with Goldwater, but Johnson consolidated the much larger "we don't want to die" voting bloc.

The British Invasion

1964 was also the year England sent one million heavily armed troops to the east coast of the United States, causing death and destruction wherever they went, in the name of Her Majesty, Queen Elizabeth.

Check that, sorry, that was left over from a different version of the century. Yes, that actually happens in one version of the century (so, again, don't make things worse).

The real "British Invasion" began when rock and roll band The Beatles appeared on The Ed Sullivan Show in November, 1964, changing the course of popular music and culture for generations to come.

By the end of 1964, The Beatles were more famous than it is humanly possible to be. This was mostly due to their looks, since no one had actually heard any of their songs yet. Audiences at concerts were so loud, and screamed with such wild abandon, that they drowned out the music. Even the Beatles themselves never heard their own songs until at least two years later.

A less bloody British invasion.

The Beatles: John, Paul, George, and Ringo, arriving in New York in 1964. Strangely, they used music and love as weapons, instead of tanks.

Throughout 1964 and 1965, Lyndon Johnson pushed an amazing collection of social and civil rights acts through congress. He initiated a "war on poverty" (which, much to the surprise of Republicans, was NOT a war on poor people, as they had hoped), and signed the 1965 Voting Rights Act into law.

Republicans were predictably upset by The Voting Rights Act, as it guaranteed all citizens the right to vote, something they were opposed to.

As the first half of the 1960's drew to a close, President Johnson seemed to be a caring, effective and thoughtful leader.

Side-note on political commentary and opinion:

We at the Guide do not want to be seen as taking sides in the historical political debate between Republicans and Democrats.

We acknowledge the pure, unadulterated bone-headedness of the vast majority of Democratic politicians, and state for the record our understanding of this bone-headedness.

It's just that the Republican Party has this historical pattern of being completely and totally insane.

In pointing out the historical fact of Republican insanity, it may at times seem as if we are taking sides and giving the Democrats a pass.

This is not our intention.

As we think will become clear in the next chapter, Democrats, even those who seem at times to be good people, often turn out to be power-hungry, dysfunctional sociopaths.

And on that happy note, it is time for all the mind-bending fun of…

The Late 1960's

By 1966, the United States was stuck in a quagmire. The country had believed, since its great victory in World War 2, that it could do no wrong.

This attitude led the United States down a rabbit hole called Vietnam.

Vietnam was a mistake. It was such a big mistake, that the word "Vietnam" came to define the sort of mistake a country should never make. Just listen to the promises before every war the U.S. got into for the next 50 years; "This will not be another Vietnam!" "We will not get drawn into any more Vietnams!" "We've kicked Vietnam syndrome once and for all!"

The fact that it was a mistake became obvious to everyone who had not gone completely and totally insane.

This was a surprisingly small group of people.

Vietnam had been fighting French colonialists for 100 years.

World War 2 had upset the balance of colonial powers around the world. The United States had won the war with its allies, England and France. After the war, England and France were eager to restore their colonial control over all the countries they controlled before the war.

For the Vietnamese nationalists, this looked like a rare chance to gain their independence, and they appealed to the Americans – who better to understand their desire for freedom and independence – to intervene and persuade the French to let go of their colonial ambition, and grant Vietnam its independence.

This all made perfect sense to the Americans, and they prevented France from re-establishing Vietnam as a colony.

Nope! By now, you can probably guess where we got that alternate history from.

A simple decision like that in the late 1940's might have prevented massive bloodshed. So, of course no one took the idea seriously.

The Americans sided with their ally, France, and set in motion a series of events that would later see America take over Vietnam from France in the late 1950's and settle into a long bloody mistake.

It all began at the end of the Eisenhower Presidency in 1959, but at the time, and through the Kennedy years, the number of troops was small enough that people could avoid paying attention.

By 1966 there were almost 400,000 American troops in Vietnam, and the country as beginning to ask, "Hey, what's this?"

When everyone finally began paying attention, the military leaders already knew it was a mistake.

So, of course they dug in deeper.

It was almost as if, once they got deep into the war and realized it was a mistake, they were too embarrassed to admit it, so they did the only thing they could think of; they stayed for a decade.

Vietnam...

Once they realized it was a mistake, they did the only thing they could think of: they stayed for a decade.

Social change and protest movements

The growing civil rights movement, which had already been around for several years by the mid 60's, along with the growing disapproval of the conflict in Vietnam, was also mixed together with new, innovative rock and roll music. All these combined elements created an environment into which social change found a comfortable new home.

The youth of the mid 1960's felt empowered to question the very foundations of the culture.

It is always dangerous to question things, to think for yourself, and to be creative in new and ground-breaking ways.

The older generation had not given the younger generation permission to think for themselves, so these kids were considered crazy, ungrateful lunatics.

They weren't…at first.

The lunacy didn't happen until an unexpected new substance was thrown into the mix; something called lysergic acid diethylamide, or LSD…"Acid," and even then it didn't create outright lunacy until the fifth or sixth….or 258th time you took it.

To fully understand the whirlwind of issues that changed from year to year, sometimes from month to month, during the late 60's, let's begin with a simple list:

-Civil Rights

-The Sexual Revolution

-Women's Rights

-The Anti-war Movement

-Drugs

-The Environmental Movement

-The birth and 'death' of "Hippie"

-Music

-Fashion

-"All You Need is Love"

-Eastern Religious Influences

-The 'Free Store'

-Landing on the Moon

-Woodstock

-Altamont

Civil Rights

The Civil Rights movement had been going on for several years already and can be considered the founding movement of the 1960's generation.

Dr. Martin Luther King, Jr. was considered the movement's leader, although other, more aggressive leaders had also emerged. Malcolm X questioned the diplomatic and non-violent methods of King. Progress was too slow, he argued.

The conflict between slow, successful progress, and the push for faster, more radical progress created a dilemma. Into this dilemma came all the old racist assholes, who eventually ended the lives of BOTH King and Malcolm X.

Olympic Athletes John Carlos and Tommie Smith in their iconic protest pose, raising their fists in a "Black Power" salute, as the national Anthem plays at the 1968 Olympics.

The Sexual Revolution

As we pointed out in an earlier chapter, sex was invented in the 1920's. There was one lingering, annoying consequence of sex, though; it got people pregnant.

The approval, in 1960, of the birth control pill, seemed to solve this problem, and allowed everyone to engage in endless, consequence-free sex for the rest of their lives (they thought in the 60's).

By the late 60's "Free Love" was a concept that had spread throughout the counter-culture movement.

People were engaging in a sexual freedom that had never been known before. New free-thinking attitudes meant that people felt free to express their sexuality without the strict moral boundaries they had been raised with.

Women felt proud of their bodies in ways they had never felt free to express before, and many felt empowered to openly flaunt their sexuality without worrying about quaint concepts like embarrassment or shame.

Men…well, unfortunately, men felt the same way.

It was natural…and beautiful and all, but let's face it, as is usually the case, once men started getting involved (and getting naked) the sexual revolution was doomed.

The Women's Movement

As great as the sexual revolution was, it was compromised by the presence of…well…men.

A growing population of free-thinking women began to question everything about the accepted social structures that saw them treated as second-class citizens.

Even the sexual revolution itself, while empowering women to take control of, and take pride in their own sexuality, too easily fed into objectification of women. It sometimes still caused women to be viewed as merely sexual objects.

Again, the blame falls totally and completely on…men.

The dueling concepts of: A) a woman being empowered to express her sexuality, and B) the truth that she is also a man's intellectual equal, were too complicated for men to keep in their heads at the same time.

Women rose up. They marched in the streets demanding equality. They expressed their freedom of thought, opinion, expression.

As with many issues in the 60's, the protestors were right.

So, of course men met secretly, discussing in long, intense debates, how the hell they could get these women to shut the hell up.

A beautiful, nearly naked "Hippie."

Beauty and equality; too many concepts for men to understand

The Anti-war Movement

Nothing brought more protestors to the streets than the increasingly frustrating war in Vietnam.

By the late 60's, as the war protestors also began embracing all the new and innovative 'lifestyle choices' of the era, war protests themselves began to take on a new and creative twist.

Exercising the newly discovered powers contained in a single flower, hippies proceeded to confuse countless police and military personnel.

Flower Power!
A young woman unleashes a flower's hidden powers, thoroughly confusing Military Police.

Eventually the unpopularity of the war spread beyond the youth. By 1968, President Johnson had become so unpopular because of the war, that he refused to run for re-election.

Richard Nixon ran on a 'secret plan' to end the war and was elected President. It turns out his secret plan to end the war was the brilliant strategy of NOT ending the war, at all, for another five years.

Drugs

We at the Guide want to be very careful how we say this. At no time has the Guide endorsed the use of illegal substances. We cannot warn you too strongly that if you travel interactively you must avoid partaking of the substances people put into their bodies during this era.

We understand, though, that you are traveling to the 1960's for a reason. You are planning to sample the hippie lifestyle. We can't stop you.

Please be careful.

A few pointers that might at least help you get through it more or less unharmed; do not take the brown acid at Woodstock. "Sex, drugs, and rock and roll" was a great slogan, but at least two of those things sent people to the hospital on a regular basis.

A common phrase used after the 60's was, "If you remember the 60's you weren't really there." It was true, and there was a reason for it.

Have we mentioned that we think all time travel should be incognito, and not interactive?

Yes? Several times? We understand each other then?

Okay, we tried. Now you're on your own.

The environmental movement

"Tree huggers"

That's what the first environmentalists were called.

Trees are For Hugging...

Along with the host of other causes capturing people's attention in the 60's, a new and growing awareness of our planet's fragile condition brought worry and concern to the fossil fuel industry.

Worried that they would not be allowed to indiscriminately rape and plunder the planet for its resources, most big corporations took the tactic of attacking scientists as 'fear mongers.'

Few new movements were more important, more vital to the future of the planet. As for the hippies who joined the new environmental movement, well, yes, they were tree huggers, literally. They hugged trees. They kissed them. People were on drugs. It was the age of free love. What more do you want to know?

The birth and 'death' of "Hippie"

Being 'hip' was one of the new measuring sticks used to decide if you were up to date on the latest trends.

If you grew your hair long, listened to the latest rock and roll music, marched in street protests, and partook of a few 'mind-expanding' substances, chances are you were starting to think of yourself as 'hip.'

In 1967, in San Francisco's Haight-Ashbury district – named for the cross streets and considered ground zero of the counter-culture – the movement had become so entrenched in local culture that a San Francisco Chronicle reporter took it on himself to name the movement. He coined the word "Hippie."

It spread quickly across the country.

In New York, where the movement still held a strong connection to the 1950's beatniks, the word "hippie" quickly took over.

Sight-seeing tour buses began taking San Francisco tourists through the Haight-Ashbury district, to ogle at the long haired 'crazies.'

The hippies themselves, never ones to skip an opportunity to entertain and surprise, staged the 'death of hippie' wake in October of 1967.

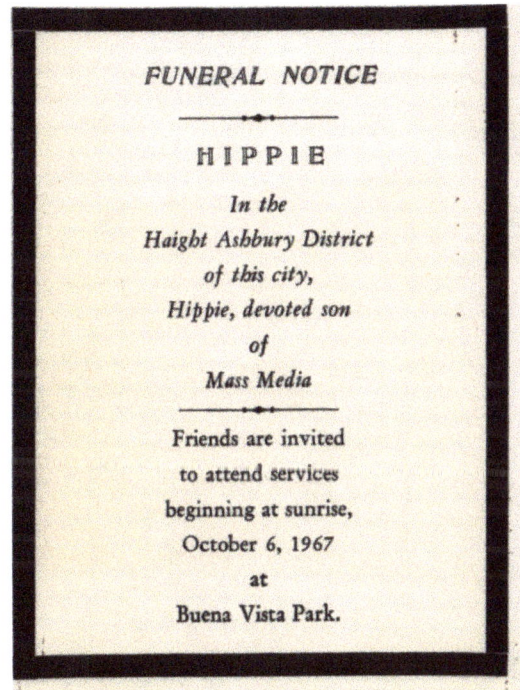

The "Death of Hippie," staged by... Hippies.

In the end the word 'hippie' stuck. It remained part of popular culture for years afterward.

Music

The early 60's "British invasion" saw bands such as The Beatles, The Rolling Stones, The Who, The Yardbirds, The

Kinks, The Animals, and countless other British musicians cross the Atlantic to conquer America. They had been weaned on American blues and rock and roll from the 1950's.

By the late 60's rock and roll music had taken the culture down new creative roads unimaginable just a few years earlier. Still at the forefront, The Beatles released "Sergeant Pepper's Lonely Hearts Club Band" in 1967. The album crystallized the new 'psychedelic' zeitgeist. Many other bands were right there with them; Jimi Hendrix, The Doors, and Janis Joplin, among others.

Parents across the nation spoke in unison, often repeating the phrase, "These kids today, with their long hair and their loud music!" It was mandatory for all parents to say this at least once a day through the 60's. Mandatory! Fines were issued if they forgot.

The Jimi Hendrix Experience, 1968.

Fashion, Eastern religions, "All You Need is Love"

As the late 60's "Counter Culture" established itself more and more as simply the "Culture," much of main stream America felt left behind.

Styles and fashion were difficult to keep up with, because they were more often anti-style, or anti-fashion.

Society also pushed back against the irreparable damage being caused by all this out of control "peace and love" stuff.

When the Beatles visited India in 1968 to study under Maharishi Mahesh Yogi, there was no telling just how much damage love and peace was going to cause. If no one stopped it, EVERYONE would start loving one another!

When John Lennon sang the iconic anthem, "All You Need is Love," there was real danger that this entire generation would turn out be a loving caring group of people. Someone in power had to stop it! If they didn't, TENDERNESS and HARMONY would spread like a malignant infection across the land!

The Free Store, Guerilla Theater

Hippies were also never ones to pass up an opportunity to shock and surprise. The Diggers was a community action and "guerilla theater" group established by, among others, Peter Coyote. The Diggers became famous in San Francisco for staging surprise performances, and for opening "Free stores," in which everything on the shelves was free to take.

This confused shoppers who wanted to shop-lift items from the store. They would sneak around pretending not to have anything hidden in their pockets. Then they would be smiled at by one of the Diggers, who knew they were hiding stuff. Then they were free to leave without paying.

Very confusing!

The Diggers joined forces with radical New York performance-art group, "Up Against the Wall Mother Fuckers," or UAW/MF.

These groups described themselves as "Community anarchists."

The UAW/MF actually forced their way inside the Pentagon during one anti-war protest in 1967.

The stage was set.

On one side you had the traditional American culture, conservative, stuck in its ways, rich, powerful, militaristic.

On the other side you had free thinkers, free spirits, activists, lovers, artists, philosophers, and revolutionaries.

Who would win?

Landing on the moon

While the culture wars raged across the country, all the smart nerdy people just kept on doing what smart nerdy people do; they sent astronauts into space.

On July 20, 1969, Neil Armstrong became the first human to walk on the moon.

It seemed appropriate, during this time of cultural upheaval, in which no one seemed to know what to think from one day to the next, that humans would actually visit a tiny piece of land on another rock in space for the first time.

There are, of course, those who believe the moon landing was faked by film director Stanley Kubrick, who amazed the world with his ground-breaking film, "2001: A Space Odyssey."

We at the Guide know exactly what happened. That's the best part about incognito time travel.

We are contractually barred from settling the argument, though. Besides, it's more fun to let the argument continue on into eternity.

We could tell you if this is really the moon, but it's more fun to let people argue.

Woodstock

Woodstock was a 3-day festival in August, 1969. Originally it was intended to be a relatively normal music festival, with tickets sold ahead of time. In the end, nearly a half million people showed up, most of them allowed in for free.

The event has become a central moment in the history of both the 60's and the larger culture afterwards. It was a watershed moment in which a huge impromptu gathering of random people were able to live, co-exist, have fun, and bring all the 60's counter culture elements together at one time, with no signs of discontent (even though the three days often saw heavy rain showers), violence, or noticeable discord.

Woodstock August, 1969.

Joe Cocker performs for Shirtless fans.

Richie Havens performs.

Attendees survive the 3-day festival in an improvised community setting.

The crowd shrugs off bad weather and brings the 60's spirit of peace and love to its 'highest' moment.

For one brief moment it looked as if the hippies were winning the hearts and minds of the country.

Then Altamont happened.

Altamont

Proving that for every yin there is a yang, four months after Woodstock, in December, 1969, a free concert was staged at Altamont Speedway outside of San Francisco, California.

The concert was envisioned by some as a "Woodstock West," and a lineup of Santana, Jefferson Airplane, Crosby Stills Nash and Young, The Grateful Dead, and The Rolling Stones was booked.

300,000 arrived for the concert, but unlike the loving and harmonious atmosphere that Woodstock had nurtured, things at Altamont turned unexpectedly violent.

The Grateful Dead refused to take the stage shortly before they were scheduled to start, and the Rolling Stones set up for the concert's final set.

Things were getting so out of control that at one point the Stones actually paused a song part-way through, while Mick Jagger pleaded with the crowd to calm down.

Added to this mix was an increasingly drunk Hell's Angels security force (they had been offered free beer all day in exchange for providing security).

As the Stones valiantly tried to complete their planned set, the crowd and the security turned on each other, resulting in the death of an audience member.

Many people feel that this was the moment when the 60's died.

Basking in all the feel-good afterglow of Woodstock, with everyone beginning to wonder if the hippies might be on to something, all it took was one more free concert, turning violent, resulting in a death, to bring the hippies' utopian hopes crashing down.

As massive as the counter-culture movement was, as revolutionary as these new attitudes were, it was all too fragile, too directionless, sometimes too excessive, and definitely too drug-fueled, to last.

Nixon was President.

The war was STILL on in Vietnam.

"Free love" had resulted in some unexpected new families to take care of.

It was time for the 1970's.

The 1970's

(Hey, they can't all be great decades!)

When the 1970's began, the hangover from the 1960's hit pretty hard.

Within the first two years of the decade, Jimi Hendrix was dead, Janis Joplin had passed on from this world, and Jim Morrison of The Doors died while taking a bath in a Paris Hotel room. Four students were shot by National Guard troops at Kent State University, while protesting the Vietnam war.

But…most important of all…The Beatles broke up.

The counter-culture movement stumbled into the new decade, sleep-deprived and dazed by years of drug use. Those who could stay awake for more than a few hours at a time tried to continue on the best they could. They protested, rocked and rolled, and did their best to advance the causes that they still fervently believed in.

For many, though, the 1970's ushered in a handful of brand new causes. The most important of these were; blow-drying that shaggy long hair into perfect Partridge Family locks, trading in all that creative experimentation and replacing it with "Hype." Also sleeping (for the first time since 1966).

Perfect Partridge Family locks, oh and the person under them is David Cassidy.

As the country zombie-walked toward the 1972 election, the foundation was laid for several years of directionless, confusing uncertainty.

Richard Nixon was re-elected in 1972, only to be caught in a convoluted scandal and cover-up named Watergate.

Watergate was a scandal involving thieves who broke into the Democratic Headquarters in the Watergate Hotel. They stole valuable information from the Democrats, and then spent the next two years bungling an amateurish cover-up. Nixon himself was involved. In 1974, Nixon became the first President ever to resign in order to avoid impeachment.

Technically, no, this is not Nixon plotting evil with Dr. Evil, but as they say, every picture tells a story....

It took many years, but finally, by the mid 70's, the Vietnam war was over. Nixon was replaced by Gerald Ford, and good music was replaced by Disco.

Everyone took a refreshing breath of polluted air and turned their brains off.

There were still artists in the 1970's who were creating brilliant work, but cultural trends were heading in divergent directions.

Rock and Roll was splitting into new sub genres; Led Zeppelin revolutionized the hard rock sound, which gave birth to Heavy Metal.

Punk was born in London (The Sex Pistols, The Clash) and New York (The Ramones, The New York Dolls).

Robert Plant and Jimmy Page, of Led Zeppelin, defined the new "Rock God" mythology of the 1970's.

Punk bands like The Clash and The Ramones fought against the glossy superficial elements that had taken over the music industry.

Disco took those glossy superficial elements and "got down" with them!

By 1976 the country was ready for a soft spoken, bland President who looked unlikely to do anything surprising. No one could handle surprises anymore.

Jimmy Carter debates President Gerald Ford in 1976. Those who watched the full debate reportedly plucked their eyes out and stabbed sharp objects into their brains.

Hollywood saw the emergence of a new generation of filmmakers who would revolutionize the movie industry. Francis Ford Coppola directed "The Godfather" in 1972, and "The Godfather 2" in 1974. Steven Spielberg's "Jaws" created a ticket buying frenzy in 1975. George Lucas gave the world the first "Star Wars" movie in 1977. Martin Scorsese shocked movie goers with the edginess of Robert Deniro's performance in "Taxi Driver" in 1976.

"Star Wars" creator, George Lucas

and Deniro as the cuddly Travis Bickle.

As President, Jimmy Carter oversaw rising prices and inflation, gas lines, and what he proudly called, "National malaise."

This is true. In 1979 President Carter gave a nationally televised speech in which he basically told the nation, "We suck."

President Carter tells the nation "We suck," and then tries to escape the White House disguised as a middle-aged jogger.

By the end of the 1970's the country had finally slept off the 60's. As people began to wake up they looked around and asked, "What the hell happened?"

No one could give them an answer.

The 1980's

By 1980, things had gotten so bad, that the United States was ready to let a Hollywood Actor try his luck at the Presidency.

What the hell! He did a movie with a chimpanzee... let's put him in charge of the nukes!

No one really knew what direction to turn, what causes to fight for, or how to morph disco into danceable electronic music.

In December, 1980 John Lennon of the Beatles was shot by a crazed gunman, punctuating the slow steady demise of all those hippie causes.

The 60's mystique continued on, though, as bands like The Who and the Rolling Stones continued to record and tour. That generation – the one The Who sang about in the song, "My Generation," was beginning to seem dated, though. New, hipper Artists like Michael Jackson (who still had his original face at that point) and Madonna were beginning to take over. In 1984 Madonna released an album titled, "Like a Virgin," and everybody laughed.

In 1984, Nancy Reagan explains to the President that Michael Jackson is a popular singer, not a magical Imp sent from Heaven to advise him.

Reagan wanted to be a tough-guy President, but there were no good places to go to war. The Cold War was still going on, but the Soviet Union was too big to attack. An attack like that would have side-effects, you know, that whole nuclear annihilation problem.

Reagan ended up finding a small Caribbean island named Grenada, with a population of only 100,000 people, and invaded it in 1983. It was a feel-good victory, and it wasn't "another Vietnam." Baby steps.

Reagan had a reputation for being forgetful and confused.

Reagan meets with Senior Advisors in 1985.

His Presidency was not without controversy, though.

Relationship with Gorbachev

During Reagan's time in office, a new leader took over in the Soviet Union. Mikhail Gorbachev took control and became popular around the world for not wanting to blow the planet up.

Reagan and Gorbachev very nearly negotiated a complete nuclear disarmament, only failing to reach agreement when Gorbachev requested that the United States also drop its planned "Star Wars" missile defense system.

Reagan was confused by this. He became worried that Gorbachev was Darth Vader in disguise and walked out of the talks.

Reagan and Gorbachev were on friendly terms, until Reagan became paranoid that Gorbachev would challenge him to a light saber battle.

Iran-Contra Scandal

The Iran-Contra scandal erupted in 1986, bringing the Reagan Administration the one thing it had been missing to that point; incompetent corruption.

The U.S. had been selling arms to its enemy Iran, funneling the profits from those arms sales to a group of military rebels in Nicaragua called The Contras.

It wasn't a very good scandal, as scandals go. Most historians don't even place it in their top ten Presidential scandals. True, it was shockingly incompetent, and adequately corrupt. Coming after Watergate, though, it seemed amateurish and uninspired. Congress advised those caught up in the scandal to go back to the drawing board and try to come up with something a little more scandalous. You're not even trying, they were told.

"Tear down this wall!"

As Reagan's time in office came to an end, he challenged Mikhail Gorbachev to tear down the Berlin Wall, a symbol of the Cold War standoff.

The wall had been built in 1961, separating East Berlin from West Berlin. The wall was torn down in 1989, bringing with it the end of the Cold War. People all over the world celebrated, except for those who made the James Bond film franchise. They continued to make Bond films, but without the diabolical Russian villains, the series floundered.

In the end the 1980's symbolized a return to good old pre-1960's unprincipled greed. "Greed is good," was one of the iconic quotes of the decade. Another famous quote that crystallized the 1980's was movie star Sylvester Stallone's famous line from the movie "Rambo," when he said, "Aaaaaaaaaaooooooooogh!" It struck just the right tone to articulate the thoughts, intelligence, and level of discourse of the culture and the time.

As the 1980's came to a close, the most notable thing that was happening was that the Cold War was winding down, and the old Soviet Union was splitting into several newly independent countries.

An optimistic spirit spread across the United States. A sense that the U.S. had 'won' the Cold War gave the population a renewed confidence. Many hoped that they could forget all the lessons they had learned during the Vietnam era, and that they could go back to being blindly self-confident and begin ordering the rest of the world around.

The 1990's

Reagan's Vice President, George H.W. Bush, was now President, and he needed his own war, so he could claim international 'street cred.'

The first Gulf War would be just the thing.

For about six months, from late 1990 to early 1991, the United States fought a war to remove Iraq from the country of Kuwait, which they had invaded in August 1990.

The U.S easily pushed Iraq out of Kuwait, but many military leaders wanted to continue on into Iraq, to remove Saddam Hussein from power.

President Bush said no, wanting to leave the madman in power for another decade. "He hasn't quite completed his despotic destruction of his country," Bush told his military advisers. "My son Jeb will become President a decade from now, and he will be able to get in and out of Iraq, without getting mired down in a long Vietnam of a war. I mean," he continued, "We've kicked Vietnam syndrome once and for all."

President Bush inspects some broken cement...your guess is as good as ours.

1992 Election

Having won his war, President Bush should have easily won re-election in 1992. What he didn't count on, though, was the double-whammy of (A) sex scandals actually helping Arkansas Governor Bill Clinton, and (B) the third-party candidacy of a real-life Hobbit named Ross Perot taking a large percentage of the conservative vote away from Bush.

It is true, Bill Clinton won the Presidency because he had sex with countless women. Voters were ready to risk the Presidency on someone who had had sex. The country had not experienced a leader capable of having sex in decades.

President Clinton poses with several appointees in 1998, prompting the entire country to ask, "Which ones you think he did it with?"

Grunge

Alternative music – a combination of punk-inspired rock and roll, mixed with sarcasm and showmanship – had been flourishing in underground scenes, throughout the United States, as a reaction to how absurd the 80's were.

This underground scene set the stage for Seattle bands like Nirvana and Pearl Jam to turn the culture on its head.

The only problem? Most of these bands never thought they would become famous, and openly resented the pressures that fame brought. The moment was short lived. Kurt Cobain, of the band Nirvana, perhaps the reigning icon of the movement, ended his own life in 1994. Other bands continued on, but the movement – powerful as it was – ended as quickly as it started.

Kurt Cobain defines an era, then ends it.

Revenge of the Nerds

For this entire century the nerdy guys of the world put up with abuse. The nerds were made fun of, had their heads shoved into toilets in countless schools from coast to coast. They were victims of psychological abuse the likes of which the world had never known.

Finally, as the 90's progressed, the nerds' secret decades-long plan was finally kicking into full gear.

The nerds had been laying the groundwork for many many years. They had slaved away in science labs after everyone else had gone to the cool parties. They experimented with dangerous solutions and unlikely inventions.

Finally, by the mid 1990's everything was ready to go. Bill Gates, Steve Jobs, Jeff Bezos, and countless other nerdy geniuses, flipped a switch.

The world began to change.

Computers began to take over.

Nerds became filthy rich.

The nerd revolution was on!

The rest of the world was powerless to resist this evil diabolical plan as it changed the way everyone did everything.

As was true at the beginning of the century, amazing new technological advances were changing the way people lived.

After an entire century of abuse, the nerds had exacted their ultimate revenge.

Everyone had to learn new skills.

All because of childhood trauma caused by endless hazing.

The change had come.

The nerds were in charge.

Steve Jobs and Bill Gates each became a billion dollars richer in the time it took to share this evil laugh.

President Clinton...uh...does a bad thing

In 1998, parents across the country had to turn off their televisions for several months and lie to their children about the power going out.

The reason? President Clinton and intern Monica Lewinski had done something horrible in the Oval Office. What they had done threatened to bring down all of western civilization. Was this some diabolical secret espionage act, you may ask? Had they secretly planted a self-destruct device in the halls of Congress? No! Even worse! They had engaged in a sexual encounter.

Perhaps it is a fitting end to this most absurd of centuries, that it seemed to go out in a blaze of absurdity.

It was true, the President had managed to get some "DNA" on an intern's dress.

Really? Was this the big story the century as going to end with?

Nothing more violent? Violence is more acceptable than sex, right?

No?

Just sex?

Well, there you have it.

Like we said…

Please, for the love of all things sane and absurd, please please please…do not make it worse!

Final Thoughts

When campers head out into the woods for a few nights, to get back in touch with nature, they are encouraged to be careful with nature; don't leave your campfire burning, don't upset the delicate balance between humans and nature. Above all, don't burn down the forest.

Unfortunately, you time travelers do not travel with this same sense of care and respect for time.

It does not take a genius to recognize that this 'history' of the 20th century that we have laid out for you in this Guide, is the most ridiculous, unlikely, and false history imaginable.

Even worse, this absurd century ended as the 21st century began. Just imagine what horrifyingly absurd things happened in the 21st century.

In fact, we are already seeing signs that the 21st century is also becoming totally ruined by careless time travelers.

Real people had to live through these events, and somehow make sense of them.

Impossible.

Travel incognito. Resist that compelling urge to time travel interactively.

Don't burn down the forest.

Don't ruin history for everyone else.

Is that too much to ask?

We don't think so....

Photo Credits:

Cover

-Titanic sinking; By Willy Stöwer, died on 31st May 1931 [Public domain], via Wikimedia Commons

Disclaimer 1

-Antarctica croquet; By NOAA (NOAA press release) [Public domain], via Wikimedia Commons

-Charlie Chaplin, Modern Times; By Taste of Cinema [Public domain], via Wikimedia Commons

Disclaimer 2

-Backwards clock; By Francisco Aliberti (Aliberti at pt.wikipedia) (Own work (Aliberti)) [Public domain], via Wikimedia Commons

-Melting clock; free clipart

1900-1910

-Wright Brothers airplane; By Wright Brothers [Public domain], via Wikimedia Commons

SF Earthquake; By W. C. Mendenhall [Public domain or Public domain], via Wikimedia Commons

Teddy Roosevelt cartoon; By Cartoonist for Brooklyn "Eagle" (Originally printed in the Brooklyn "Eagle", 1901) [Public domain], via Wikimedia Commons

-Jelly Roll Morton; By Photographer not credited. [Public domain], via Wikimedia Commons

-Scott Joplin; [Public domain], via Wikimedia Commons

1910-1920

-Titanic; [Public domain], via Wikimedia Commons

-Titanic sinking; By Willy Stöwer, died on 31st May 1931 [Public domain], via Wikimedia Commons

-Ford assembly line; [Public domain], via Wikimedia Commons

-Car in river; Model T Ford 1913, Public domain, via Wikimedia commons

-Kaiser Wilhelm; By Bain News Service, publisher. [Public domain], via Wikimedia Commons

-Hitler in car; Bundesarchiv, Bild 102-00204 / CC-BY-SA 3.0 [CC BY-SA 3.0 de via Wikimedia Commons

The Roaring 20's

-Clara Bow; By Bain News Service [Public domain], via Wikimedia Commons

-NYSE Sweeper; By Nationaal Archief [No restrictions], via Wikimedia Commons

-Chicago officials; By World Telegram staff photographer [Public domain], via Wikimedia Commons

-Al Capone; By Chicago Bureau (Federal Bureau of Investigation) - Wide World Photos [Public domain], via Wikimedia Commons

-Scott and Zelda Fitzgerald; By Kenneth Melvin Wright (Minnesota Historical Society [1]) [Public domain], via Wikimedia Commons

-Algonquin roundtable; [Public domain], via Wikimedia Commons

1930's

-migrant workers camp; By Franklin D. Roosevelt Presidential Library and Museum [Public domain], via Wikimedia Commons By Franklin D. Roosevelt Presidential Library and Museum [Public domain], via Wikimedia Commons

-Herbert Hoover; [Public domain], via Wikimedia Commons

-Franklin D. Roosevelt; By Elias Goldensky (1868-1943) [Public domain], via Wikimedia Commons

-William Powell/Myrna Loy; [Public domain] via Wikimedia Commons.

-Alf Landon; By Harris & Ewing, photographer [Public domain or Public domain], via Wikimedia Commons

Jesse Owens; Bundesarchiv, Bild 183-R96374 / CC-BY-SA 3.0 [CC BY-SA 3.0 de Via Wikimedia Commons

-Hitler hugging himself; Bundesarchiv, Bild 101I-811-1881-33 / Wagner / CC-BY-SA 3.0 [CC BY-SA 3.0 de via Wikimedia Commons

1940's

-Ship on fire; Naval History & Heritage Command [Public domain], via Wikimedia Commons

-D-Day; By Royal Navy official photographer, Russell, J E (Lt) [Public domain], via Wikimedia Commons

-James Stewart-Clark Gable; By The original uploader was Bwmoll3 at English Wikipedia (Transferred from en.wikipedia to Commons.) or CC-BY-SA-3.0], via Wikimedia Commons

-King Kong-Godzilla; By Toho/Universal Int. (Trailer for the film) [Public domain], via Wikimedia Commons

1950's

-Duck and Cover; [Public domain] via Wikimedia Commons

-Kids under desks; Walter Albertin [Public domain], via Wikimedia Commons

Howdy Doody; By NBC Television (eBay item front back) [Public domain], via Wikimedia Commons

-Joe McCarthy; By United States Senate [Public domain], via Wikimedia Commons

Early 60's

-Eisenhower; By White House [Public domain], via Wikimedia Commons

-John F. Kennedy; By White House Press Office (WHPO) (John F. Kennedy Presidential Library and Museum) [Public domain], via Wikimedia Commons

-Jackie Kennedy; [Public Domain] via Wikimedia Commons

-Johnson and MLK; Yoichi Okamoto [Public domain], via Wikimedia Commons

-The Beatles; By The_Fabs.JPG: United Press International (UPI Telephoto) Cropping and retouching: User:Indopug and

User:Misterweiss derivative work: Zakke (The_Fabs.JPG) [Public domain], via Wikimedia Commons

Late 60's

-Vietnam; By Jasen1997 (Own work) [CC BY-SA 3.0 via Wikimedia Commons

-Olympics Black Power salute, By Angelo Cozzi (Mondadori Publishers) [Public domain], via Wikimedia Commons.

-Hippie girl; By David Levine from Portland, USA (Wisdom) [CC BY 2.0 via Wikimedia Commons

-Flower Power; By Department of Defense [Public domain], via Wikimedia Commons

-Trees are for hugging; By Notnarayan (Own work) [CC BY-SA 3.0 via Wikimedia Commons

-Death of Hippie; By Diggers/Switchboard Uploaded by Grenachx at en.wikipedia [Public domain], via Wikimedia Commons

-Jimi Hendrix; By Reprise Records (eBay front back) [Public domain], via Wikimedia Commons

-The Moon; By NASA [Public domain], via Wikimedia Commons

-Woodstock (all five picture); By Derek Redmond and Paul Campbell (Own work) [GFDL CC-BY-SA-3.0 or CC BY-SA 2.5], via Wikimedia Commons

1970's

-David Cassidy; By ABC Television Network. (eBay item photo front photo back) [Public domain], via Wikimedia Commons

-Nixon; By General Services Administration. National Archives and Records Service. Office of Presidential Libraries. Office of Presidential Papers. (01/20/1969 - ca. 12/1974) President (1969-1974 : Nixon). White House Photo Office. (1969 - 1974) [Public domain], via Wikimedia Commons

-Robert Plant and Jimmy Page; By Dina Regine [CC BY-SA 2.0, via Wikimedia Commons

-The Clash; By Helge Øverås, http://www.helgeoveras.com/concertphoto.shtml (Own work) [GFDL (http://www.gnu.org/copyleft/fdl.html), CC-BY-SA-3.0 (http://creativecommons.org/licenses/by-sa/3.0/) or CC BY 2.5 (http://creativecommons.org/licenses/by/2.5)], via Wikimedia Commons

-The Ramones; By en:User:Mrhyak (Uploaded as en:Image:1983 b.JPG on March 3 2007.) [Public domain], via Wikimedia Commons

-Disco; By eeyrsja (Open Clip Art Library image's page) [CC0], via Wikimedia Commons

-Carter Ford debate; David Hume Kennerly [Public domain], via Wikimedia Commons

-George Lucas; By AP Wirephoto [Public domain], via Wikimedia Commons

-Taxi Driver; [Public domain], via Wikimedia Commons

-Carter jogging; [Public domain], via Wikimedia Commons

1980's

-Reagan on set; By General Electric [Public domain], via Wikimedia Commons

Reagan with Michael Jackson; By Pete Souza, Official White House photographer for President Ronald Reagan [Public domain], via Wikimedia Commons

-Reagan with 'cabinet'; [Public Domain] via Wikimedia Commons

-Reagan with Gorbachev; [Public domain], via Wikimedia Commons

1990's

-Bush, Sr.; By Biddle, Susan. Records of the White House Photograph Office, 01/20/1989 - 01/20/1993 (Collection GB-WHPO) [Public domain], via Wikimedia Commons

-Clinton with staff; By White House Photographer [Public domain], via Wikimedia Commons

-Kurt Cobain; By Курт Кобейн [CC BY-SA 4.0] via Wikimedia Commons

-Jobs ad Gates; By Joi Ito from Inbamura, Japan (Steve Jobs and Bill Gates on Flickr) [CC BY 2.0 (http://creativecommons.org/licenses/by/2.0)], via Wikimedia Commons

www.ingramcontent.com/pod-product-compliance
Lightning Source LLC
Chambersburg PA
CBHW051549010526
44118CB00022B/2636